I0407818

GRAVITY IN DESIGN

FLORIAN T. WOS

GRAVITY IN DESIGN

REASONING OF FORM AND FUNCTION

FLORIAN LAWOS

Dedicated to my broader family and half-cousins.

An almost perfect and self-closing circle originating from the very same place turning the world so far for everyone. Northern Berlin. Beautiful.

CONTENTS

PREFACE

In my previous and first book 'interests and it's special interests' i mostly expressed my political ideas around a more unified taxation model, narrowing aspects of life negatively influenced by corporate lobby-ism down to it's only 5 main categories to act as a counterbalance—if democratically rated on for either a slightly taxation or subsidize.

—Bridging a gap between more individual freedoms in a free market economy and at the same time allowing enough revenue required for social equality and further mutual agreement between our world's two major economical systems of capitalism and socialism.

Unfortunately, a time of circumstances and revealings in my private life and background that ended up in an incredibly hostility to delay me from finishing the title until march 2015, followed by even further hostility and incidents writing my later memoirs and assumed last words.

A tragic and complex situation—out of a few selfish interests— today still ongoing for more than 3 years, but fortunate enough for me to regain some of my abilities for a supposed 2nd book I initially intended to fuse with my understanding of cancer preventive nutrition, nutraceuticals and supplements. A broad and complicated topic I increasingly researched into due to the same circumstances and early onset of my own health situation, but successful enough to gain additional time to find further answers to my complicated life.

Writing the first introductory chapter for this supposed 2nd book, I today decided to separate the nutrition topic into a later solely health oriented title realizing the similar broader topic between evolutionary design, politics, longevity and health-aspects I initially intended had already been well written about in to many other inspiring books.

Orienting this book around my ideas related to design and life-aspects, I still hope to be allowed enough time finishing the other title afterwords. With my almost 20 year interest in 3d graphics and design in general, I also hope to gain further acceptance of my person by a certain privileged design and technology related audience.

ACKNOWLEDGMENTS

Given the previous 3 year's, I'm still grateful for every further day I feel able enough to write anything at all. Hopefully leaving at least a different perception of me besides the unsurpassed discredit around my life and family background next to the efforts continued to further prevent me by any means, injury to my brain and still ongoing hostility to this moment. Still uncertain by my currents situation if I'd ever be allowed to recover enough for the additional research required for the health oriented title, I'm grateful for every single day to pursue and especially still thankful to God alone guiding me along.

GRAVITY IN DESIGN

INTRODUCTION

There is always a certain point when a mind reaches it's final edge of sanity and reasoning, even my own. Pursuing through a few emotionally incredibly painful years, reasoning for every hope to find a place somewhere.. or anywhere and just different and distracting enough to be no longer alone. And even writing these words, it is so incredible more painful to accept that my abilities might have even further declined to no longer meet my own bottom acceptance level of quality anymore. Leaving me with not much additional to the many previous words rejected, ignored and even joked about. And it's so much I had already written before, phrased better or simply from a different angle to be impossible to add further onto. Music lyrics, my political ambitions, all dreams and aspirations I ever had.. and it all reaches back to just the same envy against me starting already in 7th grade.

Writing this—in memory of the previous hours of further certainty to likely be not alive soon—I must have finally reached a point to accept that I'd not even myself would consider me to be still human by everything I survived sane already. Incapable to even cry about it due to the injury of my brains emotional area by direct intent of a few. Additional to the only reason of knowing how all my previous ideas lead to a few certain design developments in less know fields of science, always leaving a balance between my emotional loss and the self-esteem I gained remembering more of how much i unintended helped to accomplish. Revealings by every more detailed memory from these many years. After so unsurpassed much pain I went through, it's still to this moment the only positive counterbalance left to not just break apart.

I still had so many unique ideas during these 16 isolated years, always only satisfied by new perspectives instead of working results due to the lack of drive caused by interests against me by a less known field of research, substances and oxidative stress prevented me from heading for any goals. But as unintended side effect, I adapted to mostly reading into news and technology and gained my almost native English writing abilities overs these years.

Aside from the likely most marbolous graffiti or characters I could have drawn if I ever felt driven enough by love, I instead just lost myself in my interests to find new topics or new answers for life aspects instead of impressing myself with presentable results or output. Only satisfied finding at least complete new topic each day. Every single moment I moved from the coffee-machine back to my desk, driven by any new unforeseen field study further into. Incredible hard to be explained otherwise than just a long list in searching for the 'possible best' in all fields of science. From getting a general understanding of the periodic table above just learning, further adding onto my list of efficiency and trade-offs between materials, design, mechanics and architecture. Always adding to a complete new perspective for more universal understanding adding to previous gains.

I could have achieved so much more different, specialized or visible results these years—from music to art to be shown around—instead I happened to be only driven each day to dive into new branches of technology to obtain a broader perspective of science and arts, just to distract myself from my actual work situation by any means. Fusing my younger aesthetics of graffiti with the corporate world in two additional painful years searching for the perfect in simplified web-design, interfaces, clean look, typography and spacing. Fusing my earliest interest as a kid in the works of Leonardo DaVinci with a modern understanding of design but from a new composite perspective, later even applied in related ideas. Interestingly, especially typography —a skill required to abstract form and function of characters— I started by my earliest graffiti at 11 years later literally kept me sane and alive remembering an early concept design part I had due to my early drawing interests. Understood by only so many, but well known by a certain audience.

Especially ideas are often considered only 'so much' important. Even the astonishing new and different iPhone concept later had been almost taken for granted by everyone and not even valued by manufacturers applying the design worldwide. But it's indeed the most simple but profound ideas that lead to actual breakthroughs and new paradigms in technology, a new efficiency by a new applied simplicity.

In the chapters following an introduction of design factors in nature, society and politics, I'm hopefully successful to bridge a new and different reasoning to design, beauty, style and prototyping directly. Explain an idea i had in these years in a unified approach to free-form design, further detailed by graphics in a later chapter.

GRAVITY IN LIFE

As everything in our universe obviously depends on the laws of physics and foremost gravity, a few similar universal, but less noticed laws of attraction and accumulation apply almost everywhere in nature and life—from the evolution of lifeforms to later civilized social structure.

A simple and general rule. Similar as gravity in space attracts individual colored drops of fluid into a single one—leaving an object with an even higher gravitational attraction—a similar effect of attraction and accumulation leading to an always higher influence of attraction applies to almost everywhere. From the advancement of different species throughout evolution by genetic advantages, to technical achievements leading to an individual higher advantage or influence in a social structure—at some point always universally followed by a later requirement of some form of currency as means for trade and almost automatically by the possible invention of interest and compound interest by the idea of lending in a civilized society.

Interest itself—another such similar exponential and universal law theoretically applying to any possible civilization from the first technical achievements forward—by times leading to an almost infinite accumulation of influence in our today's world just as accumulation in nature. If not restricted by other limiting factors of either room, resources, counteracting influences or policies.

In the later case just mandatory required—comparable to the rotational force in space, counteracting and allowing for balance and distance in our universe— making life, fair trade and a functional economy possible at all.

But unrelated from any scientific achievements and knowledge gained in a society, religious traditions or wisdom advancing and accumulating knowledge over time, different cultures and political structures originating from different ethnics—in this case deriving from the different geographical regions and continents formed by gravity itself—the similar laws of attraction and accumulation always apply at either some point.

A universal law as gravity itself in every aspect of nature and life, from evolutionary to technical advancements in a civilization—either as genetic or technical advantage, superiority by evolution to a higher technical efficiency or wealth gained—to formation factors of social structures, knowledge, morals, political doctrine and governing systems. Always deriving from the same universal laws of accumulation of wisdom or advancements resulting in even further influence to later developments.

A law of accumulation also applying to governing systems, only to be possibly restricted by policies intended for balance or equality or counter weight from other foreign opposing systems, but much unrelated from the underlying political doctrine. From either in a capitalistic or socialistic direction, even the most unified political system will always leave possibility for the accumulation of influence by other factors such as in-heritage of tribe, bloodline, wisdom, talent, property or wealth. From a possible most neo-liberal form of capitalism to the most equal form of socialism or policies as counterbalance for equality, either one other factor such as heritage or tribe usually leaves unequal privileges for individuals.

As a short bridge to my previous book related to influence of lobby-ism to our society, it's still interesting that unrelated from the system itself, there is always a certain balance of different interests, ethnics, cultures or stages of development and wisdom archived and similar counterbalanced by just other factors as mutual agreements or peace treaties. With an obvious exception of wars fueled solely out national or financial interests.

Besides, our already far developed world—thanks to all technical achieved interconnection and ways to travel leaving mostly all ethnic and religious differences aside—is almost in a perfect balance with the only two fundamental different political views of capitalism and socialism.

Views differing mostly only in the orientation to more or less social equality, but theoretically not far from a mutual agreement if a more unified and smarter taxation system could counteract the universal underlying law of the infinite accumulation of narrow and special interests in our western economies. A driving but often in-human force in our free market to yield innovation by a remorseless competition, on the other side highly inefficient reason for health-

and environmental related problems and social inequality.

As always, a similar equation of attraction and accumulation of interests—highly efficient as in nature—to require additional balance at some point, while at the same time reaching a hand to alternative and more human centered socialistic economical systems to allow for further mutual agreements, democracy and ongoing peace in our world. Not mandatory opposing a possible agreement to a global governmental policy in a distant future, but mandatory to counteract an accumulation of solely financial interests to leave room for a balanced ecosystem at all—just like our own solar system remains in balance by gravity counteracted by rotational forces.

But unlike my previous and first book 'interest and it's special interest' detailing a possible option for a counterbalance by taxation, I'd like to further detail some of my over the years collected reasoning applying to both design and nature the same time. Hopefully inspiring enough for other aspects of life.

DESIGN BY APPROXIMATION

The obvious answer to an often referred question, 'Form by function or function by form?' — Neither one. Both can only be approximated by reasoning between all dependencies the same time.

Nature gives birth to it's infinite sophisticated and perfect designs by each small advantage of a slight form change in the same way—the better function tested and selected by its superiority or efficiency to the already selected previous. But in evolution the beauty of new design is mostly comparable by its better adaption of the surrounding ecosystem, as general atheistic views usually contradict any 'cool factors' or personal taste the same way as reasoning in our already design and technology depended society.

Only the beauty of so incredibly many different and colorful species in nature will always leave— at least for me and with Darwin's theory still valid throughout evolution—an answer of a higher authority intending it for a reason according to the likely similar intended laws of physics.

Possibility of a higher civilization, already deriving from God's proof of love in every detail in our beautiful and perfectly balanced nature, almost self explanatory intended as a room for us, likely even room for whatever new universes we could our-self simulate in software one day. Still, above all explanations through millions of years evolution and understanding in science—the always remaining answer of a creator behind the beauty of each smallest detail as if it couldn't be any different or at least had to exist once. By the beauty of just our own color perception and colors in nature alone, every imaginable color pattern or leaf form explained by evolution's selection and influence of the laws of physics — even with all forms of perfect rectangular shapes seen in minerals and crystals— but at the same time beauty, astonishingly, unanswered.

From the largest to the smallest species and details in nature. Everything as it all just had to exist at least once somewhere contrary to just coincidence.

The likely always remaining god-given answer to our universe and existence, the beauty of everything and answer for myself surviving against all odds through a nightmare of 9 years, 3 months, and 19 days as of today. The only possible answer for design in nature to me? — God.

FORM, FUNCTION, EFFICIENCY

In our today's world new design mostly relates to what's been considered a 'new look', with only the requirement of a similar or better functionality in comparison to previous paradigms in technology. Most of them invented already centuries ago. From the first actual car, originating from the earliest wagon's defined by 4 wheels and the enclosed chassis or the bicycle defined by the a frame attached to two wheels and the required supporting handles, treat chain assembly and seat placed in their corresponding positions, to the first actual telephone as another example—

originally a box with large and curved seperate handle by it's requirement to enclose an analog speaker and membrane microphone close to the head—to the most narrowed down version in form of the first brick shaped phones. Later even further refined by the new paradigm shift the iPhone initiated to a maximum screen space oriented around a solely new interface design, thinnest and lightweight shape and newbuilt in features such as better camera or battery time. But to this day still overall abiding to the initial form-factor.

Almost a general equation from all types of mechanical solutions and tools—with a 'coffee mill' as another example— by either some form or mechanical shape deriving from a required function, enclosed by a casing or frame to support and hide the more complex mechanical structure as in most machines and power tools in our modern industrial era.

Many designs still originating from their early invention during previous centuries as mostly everything of either transport or machinery we know. Only further enhanced from aesthetic aspects later on, up to the era of computer aided free-form design and plastic casting intended for a modern and clean outside look, yet on the inside revealing the typical and less aesthetic gratings and material savings.

FRAMES AND STRUCTURES

Nature gave birth to the most efficient frame-structures throughout evolution by selection of a higher tensile strength to weight ratio as an advantage to survive for certain species. Mutations—according to Darwin—lead by coincidence to lighter bones and in return offered a superiority using less energy to move faster and gather food. Less affected by gravity, and therefore the advantage of faster speed and strength to survive. In plant species a better resistance to harsh weather conditions, using less minerals and resources to grow and prosper fast. Selection, as discovered by Darwin, millions of years from seashells and riffs building faster, leading to structures with the smallest amount of minerals required to sustain the harshest conditions of gravity and weather. Less breakage by the highest strength to weight ratios and therefore leading over time to the most efficient selection of structure patterns throughout nature.

Bones, with the lightest porous and efficient minerals structures, trees and leafs with the highest longitunal tensile strength to sustain weather and animals, perfectly adapting the most efficient patterns possible by the law of molecular structures. Especially the longitunal structure of trees and weeds with it's many layers, inspiration to bundles of tubes used everywhere in architecture and composite frames. With the sophisticated porous structure of bones already well researched for architecture, medicine and other new appliances.

Leaving this only short part about evolution, already well better detailed by Darwin and other inspiring authors, I'll try to bridge over the actual design topic of this book. Beauty, aesthetic and look—but function not considered any less and above ideas to simply adapt proven designs from nature.

SIMPLICITY AND SHAPES

Clean and timeless design— by it's modern simplicity often in contrast to detailed and complex shapes in nature— requires an entire opposite approach of reasoning between a likely desired timeless look first, and then approximating a form-factor to the required functionally.

By many times misapplied to objects that ended up just futuristic by a free-form designs plastic exterior, instead of the most appropriate form and material selected by reasoning. Many such designs —for example a water heater—are seen everywhere with formed plastic casings, often with a short lifespan and large spaceful greasy material sections on the inside. In this case, a design that should originate from an easy clean-ability at first—therefore implicating only glass or ceramic as lining material with rounded corners —and then a simplified and easy to clean heating section. In this example, I came only across a single glassware manufacturer offering a timeless, transparent design of a glass-made cooker with no visible heating spirale, compared to the average cheap plastic products collecting chalk on the inside. Another approach, asking where heat might be used elsewhere in the kitchen leads to the alternative using either the microwave or griddle instead, but with a drawback to require both more energy and attention. From this point, convenience reasons back to a dedicated water heater with docking place in either some way—if not built-in into a coffee machine or water outlet already—but another good example of smart design in household appliances.

In the following chapters I'd like to detail a few of my learnings from a broader perspective of hierarchy in design, often providing a complete new answer by only a different order of questions asked.

UNIVERSE'S GEOMETRIC LAWS

Above everything else what's been considered 'new design' in it's long own evolution throughout our industrial age, there are still a many interesting principles of just our 3 dimension and gravity itself providing new answers if just focused enough on them.

The most common geometrical shapes of our 3 dimensions—and with only my own basics in math considered— circle/sphere, triangle/tetrahedron, square/cube, pentagon and hexagon—are usually explained by math alone, with the exception that the sphere, triangle, tetrahedron and hexagon shapes derive in it's geometrical definition directly from the laws of gravity itself, implicating a way higher potential and efficiency compared to the more artificial geometrical shapes.

From a single solid sphere —formed by gravity— and attracting two other ones, defining the universal form of a triangular alignment, directly followed by the most universal tetrahedron attaching another one.

3+1 — The universally highest efficient interconnecting alignment, shortest possibly interconnection everywhere in our universe and one of mostly only two alignments of many similar sized round objects in free space. If forced to an even ground surface, the similar law further defines a hexagonal shape if a single sphere if space-less surrounded by 6 additional ones.

From these exact boundary forces in physics, inspiring to the appliances in triangular crane frames, bridges and steel structures and it's similar counterpart of the nature famous and efficient honeycomb's hexagonal structure—in this case only leaving each 3rd interconnection out—seen by carbon atoms forming 'graphene', the highest tensile strength material known today, and already discovered as the likely highest tensile strength material in our universe. The universal law of tri- and hexagonal micro-structures, already well studied due to their efficiency in composite-appliances in motor-sports and other fields.

BEYOND FREE-FORM DESIGN

The initial idea behind this book originates from a time I had researched in a new composite material by rumors of new fabric material used for an upcoming iPad. Interested in a possible use for a flying car concept I had drawn before, I researched into 'ultra high molecular weigh polyethylene' —next to graphene one of the lightest materials by tear strength and about 3 times lighter than carbon fiber— to be mixed with carbon fibers already applied in composites and motor-sports. As it turned out, the patent only circumvented the use of composite materials, yet 'the lightest strength' with 'the lightest stiffness' for the ultimate possible lightweight efficiency lead me back to an earlier interest in lightweight magnesium alloys. A material I had proposed for a device's casing in a tech company before. Originating from the same time, thinking about how to apply rapid prototyping for the project, I later ended up with a different idea how to simplify design directly. Pretty much due to my biggest deficit agreeing on a final design shape by too much perfectionism. At first considering curved plates to cut the chassis from—further understanding that curve angles always derive as a subsection from a circles size—but then inspiring me to the broader idea of prototyping in the following chapter.

INTERSECTIONS AND CURVES

Interestingly the intersections for the chassis revealed another such universal law in geometry —by the possible intersection of any shape always defining a new cut section, allowing for all sorts of unique curves—but making the process similar complicated to general casting forms by the precision required for the cutting plan.

But then it appeared more easy if the sections could share the same unified curve angle, with only another set of curved plates required for the straight parts of the doors.

(picture)

Narrowing it down to concave plates with a large 3-degree curve angle—known from most sports cars roof, front section and windshield— and another set of straight sheets with the same 3 degrees for the sides sections. Still leaving the freedoms by more unique curves defined from the cutouts, it appeared that even the entire chassis could be manufactured directly this way, and with no exceptions.

A new approach, directly attaching the unified curved chassis—with another aspect to look more uniquely perfect from all angles—to the most lightweight frame of composite extrusions with the same curve angle.

BEYOND 3D PRINTING

Further inspired by 'lego tech' building kits—a set of straight parts and interconnecting joints—known for straight shapes already, only in a modern way to allow the beauty of modern sports cars and other design. It later lead me to an idea of a direct 3d application's plugin to support the new design process directly—but unlike a more time consuming 3d printing—ready to be immediately cut out and joined together. Further narrowing it down to a set of only 3 different sheet types of concave, bend extrusion and straight sheets, as well as 3 different frame extrusion and 3 different materials.

FRAMES AND FABRICS

Known by the same understanding of nature and physics, the always most efficient shape structure is defined by a most lightweight, inter-connected and stiff frame with a supported exterior hull to cover the shape.

In history, Leonardo Davinci's famous flying machine and concepts became the earliest inventions known today already applying this understanding by natures design from birds, but already in a most efficient way of many lightweight wooden spares covered with a lightweight airtight fabric for the wings. To this day, still applied similar in modern airplanes aluminum fuselage. Interestingly also an inspiration someone had together in a discussion with me, leading to a modern ultralight wing suit concept—Iron Man v3.0... after I already concepted a v2.0 version in cf.

Similar design already considered in car concepts covered only with fabric, but more difficult to archive the same aesthetics of hard surfaces. Only in most industrial designs the frame aspect became a subset of sheet metal design and often resulted in casings less efficient in their structure, easily to dent and deform, with most more efficient understandings only applied lately.

The actual macbooks unified body—with a frame structure of thin internal spares left by the CNC milling process became one of the newer approaches adapted throughout the industry, but still to be further adapted in other fields. An aspect of design behind of many household tools, from washing machines to microwaves that could be less prone to receive dents, and still add to the overall energy saving for recycling if further produced from a common aluminum fused alloy in a future.

Again, a similar universal set of principles of nature and physics—narrowing down to foremost gravity and it's deriving universal geometries, next to Einsteins brilliant equations of mass to requiring more energy to move— inspiring to lightweight design. Narrowing many considerations down to lightweight's efficiency, a triangular/honeycomb spare structure supported surface and new appliances for composite fabrics.

CONCRETE EXTRUSIONS

By the same inspiration of nature—understanding the hollow fiber structure of plants for the highest longitunal strength—a set of different new appliances offers itself for architectural use.

Extrusions from concrete—bundling together similar hollow—offer by the accumulating surfaces tear strength new appliance for larger and more unique building structures, without relying on steel frames. Additional to supporting grids of steel in concrete plates, an even higher strength by everything applied together. New appliances for large curved architecture, deriving from many fiber supported layers of concrete cured in a large convex forms. Already used sparely in modern curved architecture due to the higher cost compared to older proven methods. But similar to a new approach in car design, large curved glass surfaces only rarely seen become a new possibility if efforts are spent into large vacuum forming as a new standard for architecture, additional to usual large glass sheets already manufactured.

AFTERWORDS

literally.

— Florian

First Draft Published, March 3, 2017

ISBN-13: 978-1544045139